Let's Read!

- Read the Page
- Read the Story
- Game
- Yes
- No
- Repeat
- Stop

Fancy Nancy

Explorer Extraordinaire!

Everything in this book is scientifically accurate. (That's a fancy way of saying it's all true.)

Written by Jane O'Connor · Illustrated by Robin Preiss Glasser

For Ellie Rose, who soon will have a little sister to go exploring with
—J.O'C.

For Jeanne Hogle: Art Director Extraordinaire, with love
—R.P.G.

Photos: page 12: © Gynane/Dreamstime.com; page 15: © David Gaudry/Dreamstime.com; page 16: monarch: © Yanik Chauvin/Dreamstime.com; red admiral: © Geoffrey Kuchera/Dreamstime.com; swallowtail: © Krzysztof Wiktor/Dreamstime.com; page 18: butterfly: © Michael Gray/Dreamstime.com; moth: © Eric Isselée/Dreamstime.com; page 20: forget-me-not: © Emilia Stasiak/Dreamstime.com; foxglove: © Dole/Dreamstime.com; ladyslipper: © Alan Dyck/Dreamstime.com; Queen Anne's lace: © Scott Pehrson/Dreamstime.com; page 23: pigeon: © Ricardo André Alves/Dreamstime.com; robin: © Krzysztof Wiktor/Dreamstime.com; sparrow: © Michael Komm/Dreamstime.com; page 27: elm leaf: © Nguyen Thai/Dreamstime.com; Ginkgo leaf: © Stephane Benito/Dreamstime.com; honey locust leaf: © Alina Isakovich/Dreamstime.com; maple leaf: © Samantha Grandy/Dreamstime.com; page 28: © Ivan Zahlebin/Dreamstime.com; page 29: © Jill Battaglia/Dreamstime.com.

Bonjour, everybody!
Welcome to our club!
Bree and I love to go exploring
in the wild. We collect leaves,
watch birds and butterflies, and
inspect insects. If you're like us,
then you can be an Explorer
Extraordinaire too!
Love,
Nancy
Indelible

Bree and I are the founding members of our club. (That means we started it.) So far we are the only members.

Freddy and my sister really want to join. We say maybe. First they have to prove they are mature enough. (Mature is fancy for acting grown up.)

WHAT DOES AN EXPLORER EXTRAORDINAIRE NEED?

ESSENTIAL

Long-sleeve shirt and pants (so ticks can't get on you)

Notebook and pen for writing field notes

Baseball cap or sun hat

NOT ESSENTIAL

Camera

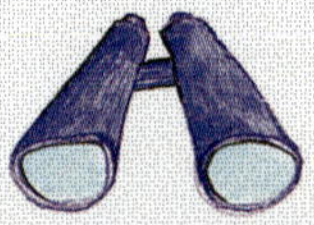

Binoculars

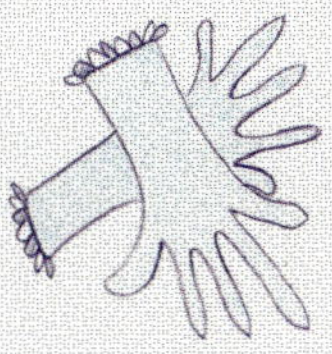

Lace gloves

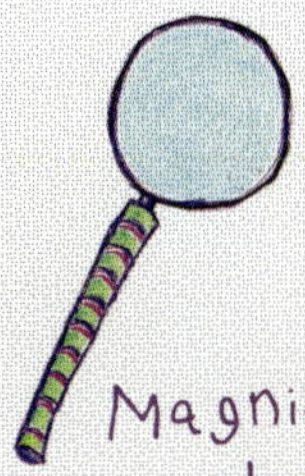

Magnifying glass

Glamorous sunglasses

Rusty

Little maracas for when we feel like dancing

Frenchy

Just because you're exploring doesn't mean you can't be fancy!

I almost forgot the most important thing.

Every club needs a clubhouse. It's absolutely essential.

HERE IS A MAP OF OUR TERRITORY.

(That's fancy for the places where we can go.)

Rule #1

We only go exploring in our backyards and Mrs. DeVine's yard.

gate
honey locust tree
rope swing
use!
Vegetable garden
Ginkgo tree
wildflower garden
oak tree
herb garden
porch
op
Mrs. DeVine's house
DeVine

Rule #2

Nobody in the club thinks bugs are gross. (That's just immature, which is fancy for babyish.)

First we look for insects. *Insect* is the real word for bug. All insects have wings, antennae, and six legs. We see an anthill. So we sprinkle some sugar.

Voilà! Here come the ants!

Ants love sweet things. (Me too!)

The ants go marching one by one. Hurrah! Hurrah!

What do you call a one-hundred-year-old ant?

An antique. (That's a fancy word for something really old.)

Rule #3

No touching; just looking.

Ants live underground in a group called a colony.
Freddy wants to help the ants get back home.
But that's against club rules.

My sister scribbled here.
She thinks it's real writing.

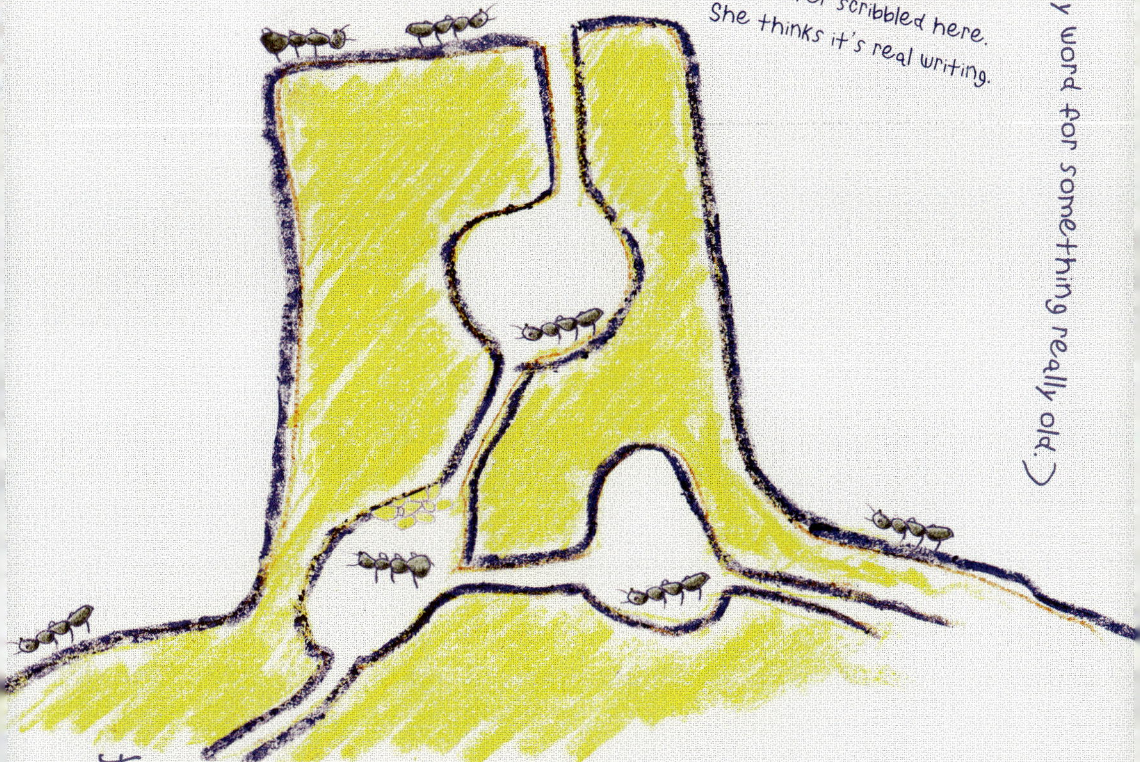

The head ant is the queen, but she doesn't have a crown or anything fancy. She lays all the eggs.

We see lots of **flies** by the garbage cans.
They zoom around so fast, Bree couldn't get a picture.

Flies can walk on ceilings
because of sticky pads
and tiny claws on their feet.

I observe (that's a fancy word for watch) a ladybug on a leaf of a tomato plant. This ladybug has one black spot on each wing. Once, I saw a ladybug with black wings and red spots. Mom says it's good luck if a ladybug lands on you. But club members do not think that is scientifically accurate.

Ladybugs eat insects that are bad for plants.

LADYBUGS I HAVE SEEN

My sister is pointing at something. It is a spider. In the web there is a dead bug. My sister says, "Yuck." But we explain that this is just part of nature. Spiders eat insects that are pests, like flies.

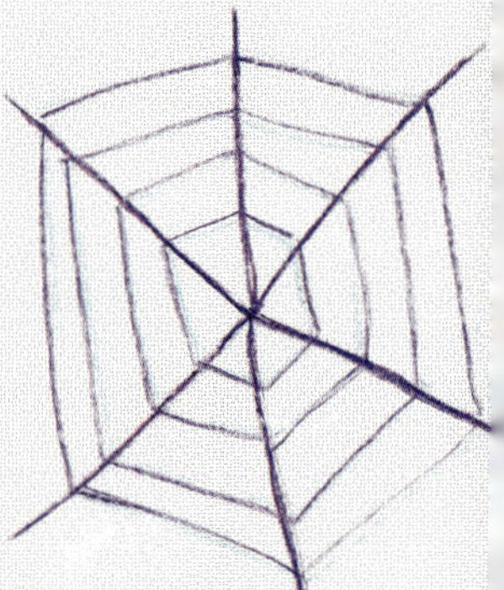

You probably think spiders are insects.

But guess what?

They're not.

They have eight legs—not six—and no wings or antennae.

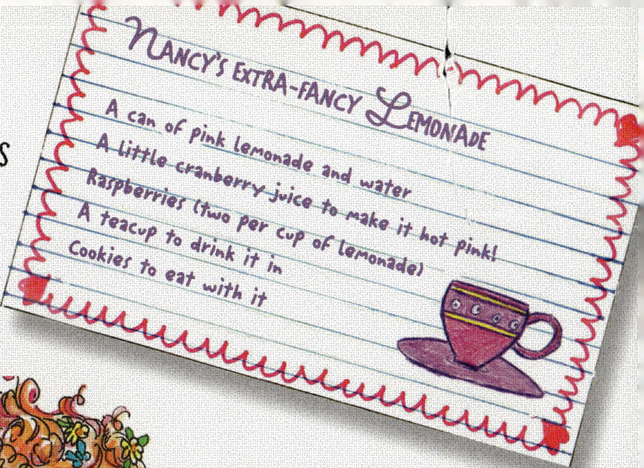

Exploring in the wild makes us very thirsty and hungry. So we need to stop and have refreshments! (That's fancy for snacks.)

Orb-spider

We do some research now. That means we read about what we've seen. Bree's book says we saw an orb-spider. Here is the photo Bree took of it.

Rule #4

Crying is not allowed (unless there is a very good reason).

My sister and Freddy fight over the last cookie. We tell them if they want to go with us to Mrs. DeVine's garden, they'd better stop.

Mrs. DeVine's flower garden is full of butterflies. Bree and I adore butterflies.

A monarch butterfly

This is a giant swallowtail

And this one is a red admiral

I TOOK THESE PICTURES.

Rule #5

We never catch butterflies because they are fragile. (That's a fancy way of saying they get hurt easily.)

Many people don't think butterflies are insects because they are so pretty.

But guess what? They are insects!

All butterflies start from an egg that turns into a caterpillar. The caterpillar spins a cocoon around itself. The scientific name is chrysalis—I think that word is so beautiful and fancy! And when the chrysalis breaks open—voilà! There's a butterfly.

I will probably be a lepidopterist when I grow up.

(That's fancy for a scientist who studies butterflies.)

LOOK-ALIKES

IS IT A BUTTERFLY?

- When butterflies land on something, their wings stay up.
- You see butterflies during the day.
- They have colorful wings.

OR

IS IT A MOTH?

- When a moth lands, its wings stay flat.
- You see moths much more at night. (They like to fly near lights.)
- A lot of moths have plain brown wings. But some moths are very colorful.

BUTTERFLY-HUNTING ENSEMBLE

I went to a butterfly farm once with my grandparents. If you go to one, here's what you should wear:

Part of Mrs. DeVine's garden is for **wildflowers**.
Wildflowers grow all by themselves without any help from people.
You don't have to buy seeds or anything.

Lots of wildflowers have such fancy names!

Forget-me-no

Ladyslipper

Foxglove

Queen Anne's lace

Oh no! Look what Freddy and my sister did. They picked some flowers without asking. That is strictly against club rules. Mrs. DeVine is not mad, but we are. Neither of them can be in the club—they are not mature enough!

LUNCHTIME!

My mom takes my sister and Freddy home. We go to Bree's house, and after lunch we will check the bird feeder in her backyard. Maybe some birds are having their lunch.

Cookie-Cutter Bird Feeder

YOU NEED STALE BREAD, COOKIE CUTTERS, YARN, AND A STRAW.

Make cookie shapes from stale bread with your cookie cutters. With a straw, make a hole in the bread. Tie yarn through the bread. Now hang your bird feeders in the branches. The tree will look like a Christmas tree for birds!

Pinecone Bird Feeder

YOU NEED PEANUT BUTTER, A PINECONE, CORNMEAL, BIRDSEED, AND WIRE.

Smear peanut butter all over a pinecone. Roll it in a mixture of cornmeal and birdseed. Ask a grown-up to wrap a wire around the top. Hang it high in a tree so other animals can't get at the bird.

Bree may be an ornithologist when she grows up. That's a scientist who studies birds.

WHAT MAKES BIRDS SPECIAL?

Birds are the only animals with feathers. (The fancy word for feather is plume.) They also have light, hollow bones. One of the reasons we can't fly is because our bones are too heavy—and we don't have wings.

Today we see a robin and lots of sparrows.

Pigeon

Sparrow

Robin

Why do hummingbirds hum?

Because they don't know the words. (Tee-hee!)

It starts to drizzle, so we go back to our clubhouse. We pretend not to see Freddy and my sister. We read about hummingbirds and learn many facts that are fascinating (that's even fancier than interesting).

HUMMINGBIRD—the official bird of our club

THEY LOVE RED FLOWERS.

So far we have only seen hummingbirds at the zoo, but they are still our favorite birds. Why?

- They are so petite (that's French for little), and their wings are iridescent (that's a fancy word for shiny).
- How petite is a hummingbird?
  - Without feathers, most are the size of a bumblebee!
  - They can take a bath in a leaf.
  - A nest is the size of a walnut shell . . . and their eggs are smaller than jelly beans.
- They flap their wings up to two hundred times a second—amazing!
- They don't hum. A humming sound comes from their wings beating so fast.

Rule #6

We don't pull leaves off trees. Trees need them to make food.

The rain seems to be stopping, but we wear our raincoats anyway because we look so chic (that is French and fancy for fashionable). Goody! The storm last night has knocked off leaves for us to collect.

Elm

I am practically a leaf expert.

Trees whose leaves fall off are called deciduous—I love that fancy word almost as much as chrysalis. (See the pages on butterflies.)

Honey locust

Maple

All the leaves here come from trees in our backyards.

Ginkgo leaves look like fans. Mrs. DeVine makes tea from the fruit.

Ginkgo

Trees with leaves that don't fall off are called evergreens—ever green, get it? The leaves look like needles. Christmas trees are evergreens. Don't you love their wonderful aroma (that's fancy for smell)?

Evergreens all have pinecones.

Once I painted a big one gold and glued on glitter—gorgeous!

Lavish Leaf Crown

You need leaves, glue, glitter, tape, and construction paper.

Cut a paper crown from a piece of construction paper. Make the strip of the crown long enough to fit around your head. Tape the ends together. Put some glue on pretty leaves. Glue on glitter. Tape or glue leaves onto crown. Voilà!

A SELF-PORTRAIT

(That's a picture of me drawn by me!)

Bree and I hear Freddy and my sister calling us.
They found something—something exciting.

Wow! They have found a baby robin!
It has fallen from its nest.

Baby robins

We can see the nest. The mother robin must be frantic! (That's fancy for very, very worried.) We call my mom and she knows just what to do. She puts the baby back in the nest. Now it is safe. My mother explains that some animals won't care for their babies after a person has touched them. But birds aren't like that.

Hooray for Mom!

My sister and Freddy jump up and down. "Please, please, can't we join the club now?"

Even though they broke some club rules, they did find the baby robin, which is the most exciting thing we observed. So Bree and I take a vote. . . .

It's unanimous! We both vote yes. We make official cards for the new members. Just like us, they are now Explorers Extraordinaire.

BIG,
SMALL,
SHORT,
TALL

BIG, SMALL, SHORT, TALL
by LOREEN LEEDY
HOLIDAY HOUSE
NEW YORK

Printed in the United States of America
First Edition

Library of Congress Cataloging-in-Publication Data

Leedy, Loreen.
Big, small, short, tall.

SUMMARY: A variety of performing animals introduce thirteen pairs of opposites such as first-last, hot-cold, and up-down.
1. English language—Synonyms and antonyms—Juvenile literature. [1. English language—Synonyms and antonyms] I. Title.
PE1591.L38 1987 428.1 86-46203 6.95
ISBN 0-8234-0645-8

FOR LISA

LAST

FIRST

DIRTY

CLEAN

HAPPY

SAD

IN

OUT

NEAR

FAR

HIGH

LOW

EMPTY

FULL

HOT

COLD

OVER

UNDER

BIG

SMALL

UP

DOWN

SHORT

TALL

FAT

THIN